UNDER THE POWER OF ETERNAL TENGRI

Erdenebat Zorig

Published by Erdenebat Zorig, 2024.

While every precaution has been taken in the preparation of this book, the publisher assumes no responsibility for errors or omissions, or for damages resulting from the use of the information contained herein.

UNDER THE POWER OF ETERNAL TENGRI

First edition. March 11, 2024.

ISBN: 979-8224424160

Written by Erdenebat Zorig.

Table of Contents

May the Mongolian Motherland revive and prosper under the power of the Eternal Heaven, and may Mongolians be full of physical, mental and spiritual energy.

May the Power of the Eternal Heaven bless Great Mongolia!

UNDER THE POWER OF ETERNAL TENGRI

MEDITATIONS ON MONGOLIAN SPIRITUAL PHILOSOPHY

By Erdenebat Zorig

Acknowledgements

Thank you very much to my wife and son for allowing me to finish writing this book.

I would like to thank Munkhtur Luvsanjambaa, an artist, writer, poet, and designer, who illustrated the cover of my book, and Bayarkhuu Jantsan, a writer who red, edited, and reviewed the Mongolian language version.

I would like to express my gratitude to my fellow readers, artists and friends who have inspired me to write this book, who has always asked for my book, who have lived and worked with me in Mongolia and abroad for many years.

I want to thank Suzannah Schmid - who has been part of my getting there; she supported, cheered and encouraged me almost every day while I was writing this book.

Thank you, Suzy!

May the Mongolian Motherland revive and prosper under the power of the Eternal Heaven, and may Mongolians be full of physical, mental and spiritual energy.

May the power of the Eternal Heaven bless Great Mongolia!

Live Under the Power Eternal Tengri!

Foreword

First of all, I would like to remind my readers that this book is not an academic research book. I wanted to write in that way, and I was "afraid" that if I did this way, it would not be beyond the reach of a few scholars and can not reach the general public. We Mongolians today need a reborn spiritually, values, and morality.

The beginning of such a rebirth is the return to the old philosophy of "well-forgotten" or "made forgotten". This book is a spiritual philosophical essay.

But let me briefly describe the path I have taken so far:

1. I realized that the beginning of the Eternal Heaven was closely connected with the shamanic rites, worship, and meditation of the Mongols. It has been established that it can affect or heal people or animals and that it can be "endangered." I decided to try it, prepared a drum, and practised for a while. Then I realized in real life that even if a person can't serve and influence a probe, it can be very influential in his body, mind, and spirit.

1. I discovered that the Eternal Heaven was a religion. During and after the Great Khan's reign, the Munkh Tengri was worshipped as "god" and imagined it as a paradise in the next realm of the universe, where the Mongols worshipped "godly" and went after death. Gerelbaatar, an Inner Mongolian researcher living in

Japan, has done a very detailed study on this. You can easily find out what he studied on the Internet, so I don't need to spend much time here. I do not agree with his attempt to over-religious this view in the past and apply it today. If this is the case, many more "monks" and "shamans" will be born, and the business of the mediators who connect man and heaven will flourish, and the deceivers will take advantage of the Mongols' beliefs and enslave their minds is alarming. Besides, we live in an era of astronomy, interplanetary flight, and information technology, not 13th- and 14th-century "horse-riding" warriors, so it's good to keep up with the present times. Religions and religious sects could shape and create. No one knows that a society that follows a religious ideology is always stagnant and backward. Therefore, it is not permissible to propagate the idea of Munkh Tengri as a religion!

1. I grew up in a society where I was educated, educated and brought up in science, technology, philosophy and logical thinking from an early age. The idea to write this book was based on one question: - Do we Mongolians have a philosophy? During his many years of work, study, and life in the west, like many other Mongolians, I was constantly thinking about the fate of Mongolia. I was always thinking about the fate of Mongolia.

What is the current situation in Mongolia? What helps them to thrive, and what prevents them from doing so? These thoughts are always ingrained in my heart. Do we Mongolians have a philosophy? If so, what could it be? If not, why not? Beliefs and worldviews play an important role in the destiny of both individuals and nations. Different countries and civilizations have different philosophies. Western European philosophy, including French philosophy, German and British classical and modern philosophy, and the philosophy of the next generation. Islamic countries have a rich philosophical tradition. Everyone knows that our southern and northern neighbours, China and Russia, have their philosophies. Mongolian philosophy is what most people call Buddhism. It's hard to say that Buddhism is not our philosophy, and it's hard to say it is. This is because all the religions and philosophical currents that were widespread at that time during the Mongol Empire entered Mongolia, and many religious teachers and philosophers lived in Mongolia at that time. However, the third way I am proposing has not been easily accepted by the people, and they are still sceptical ... When I shared my idea of a possible Mongolian philosophy with my relatives, friends, and people far away, some said, "I need to write! " Some say, "Is it useless? " Friends who say, "We need to write," They say, "Yes, we should have our philosophy as a whole nation." If there is such a thing, it should be written and passed on to future generations. "Don't write," said some people. These "Don't write," people: "Everyone has their philosophical views throughout their lives." It can be a life experience. Or it may be a systematic philosophical knowledge inherited from someone or academic way.

Even writers, poets, artists, and scientists each have their world, believe in it, interpret the world through it, and incorporate it into their work, so there can be no such thing as a unified philosophy.

Some people even directly opposed the writing of this book. Are you trying to impose an ideology on Mongolians?! They said. After Mongolians broke away from the "religions" of Buddhism, socialism, and communism, it was up to individuals to decide for themselves what to believe, what to accept as true and false, and how to look at the world from different angles! Last 30 years religious sects and political parties have sprung up in Mongolia. They all have their philosophy and ideology. It is up to the individual to decide. In addition, various esoteric and occult groups and meditation centres are competing to win the hearts and minds of Mongolians. Everyone chooses their own beliefs, convictions, and worldviews. That's why the fun less than one unified philosophy is over! Instead of wasting your time on such things, you should write and translate your literature. I have been explaining to these people as follows: - When we talk about life and national philosophy, we are talking about spirituality. No one knows that the talk of spirituality or human divinity is often used in religion, and even in the practice of worship, meditation, and prayer. It can be the worship of Christ, the Buddha, Allah, the Blessed Virgin Mary, Satan or the Devil, black and white shamans, and monks. Of course, it seems pointless to talk about National Philosophy. But that is not the case. The Nation's Government must have its ideology. It is the philosophy of the nation's centuries-old life - the experience of struggle, the worldview, the "big picture" of the world. It is about this big picture that I present to you the results of my research, study, reflection, and meditation. It is expressed in terms of a general, multifaceted "picture", "Eternal Heaven – Munkh Tengri", "The Power of Eternal Heaven – Munkh Tengeriin Huch", "The Law of Eternal Heaven– Munkh Tengeriin Huuli", and under them, "Life - Amidral" that changes, transforms, and flourishes.

Finally, if you, the wise reader, reflect on what I have to say as you review the book I am presenting to your sacred mind, and share your thoughts, the author will gladly accept it and will be able to walk that path for many years to come.

Beliefs – Worldviews

Some countries believe that society, nations, and individuals do not need to have a unified worldview, belief system, or ideology. The number of such people is increasing day by day in Mongolia. To justify this, they speak of the rights and freedoms of the individual and say that the individual must have his views, separate from society. The world is entangled in complex processes. Anything can happen at any time. It is extremely difficult to know the perspective of the process and when it will begin and end. No one knows how things will turn out. It seems impossible to guess. Therefore, it is common for most people to be limited by their own life experiences, household knowledge, and information.

In this chaotic world, humankind has always asked itself whether there is a common pattern and an overview. Each nation has its answer. This is their orientation in this world. The test of how true it is Life itself. The struggle itself. That is why we need to develop and improve our worldview and philosophy. Since there is a general picture of the world, there will inevitably be talk about beliefs. Belief is a torch and light in the darkness. When a person acts or makes a decision, he or she relies on proven knowledge and opinions about the situation.

It is a test of that person's beliefs. If it is based on false information and knowledge, the probability of achieving the goal is zero. Therefore, belief is one of the most important things in human activity.

Belief is a key driver of the real process. This belief will become an ideology. Then it is spread in the society consciously, purposefully and by the power of the state. Under that belief, under the same banner, the whole of society can unite, be led, guided, exist, prosper, and move forward together by exchanging intellectual and material cultures with humanity. There is also an ideology that contradicts the common views and values of mankind and makes people inhuman - communism, capitalism, materialism, liberalism, etc. These ideologies were good but attempt to implement them weakly made them impossible to implement.

Does anyone have to be more convincing than anyone else? Isn't it If I asked, there will be few who will say that there must be no faith. Here is a brief discussion of what belief is and how it is used in everyday life. Beliefs. This is a very important topic.

Because it is hard to walk in the dark without a flashlight, a map in the jungle, or at least a compass. If he had it all in his hand, he would have nothing to worry about, and he would continue on his confident journey. Beliefs are a guide to life. It's not a goal, it's a tool. You can aim to gain credibility. It is part of the spiritual quest. You can study books, religions and philosophies. In the end, if you don't use it to get through the deep ravines, rivers, and steppes of life, it's obvious that you don't need any beliefs.

We share our life experiences with our children. We try to pass on to our children the experiences and beliefs of our own lives and beliefs. All of this is sometimes met with opposition, indifference, and disapproval. This is because life has already changed and the beliefs that have shaped the lives of a generation are outdated. If beliefs change like this, why write a book about a particular belief? You might ask. Beliefs and thoughts about the times or the realities of society must change. It would be a different matter if the understanding of the nature of the world, the purpose and meaning of human life, developed from generation to generation, enriched with new meanings, and became a universal torch for the individual and the nation! Belief is very important! Beliefs allow a person to do and accomplish things. We know from experience that a person cannot move forward without faith.

A child who does not know that fire is hot will not hesitate to catch a hot spark, but when he learns that it is hot, he will be convinced that it cannot be touched. Modern science, including neuroscience, which studies the human brain, does not yet know how a person knows the world, how he or she acquires knowledge and information. In any case, a knowledge that has been proven, applied, and tested in practice is the foundation of any person's beliefs.

The knowledge and information that is used and tested is the foundation of any person's beliefs. For example, the science of astro physics has shown that the sun as a whole is the "pan" of hot nuclear reactions. Some believe that knowledge and belief are different. This is because superstition is equated with belief. Beliefs are formed as a result of a person's serious and well-founded knowledge of phenomena. So knowing and blindly believing are two different concepts. In addition, there are always two people who have good faith and scepticism. Beliefs, and only proven beliefs, allow a person to have the courage to take action. Therefore, the most important thing is to have an accurate picture of the world. This book is an attempt to share with you the beliefs I have developed over the years and applied in my work and life. I thought it might be useful for people of the same faith as me. If these people reflect on what is being said here in their minds and hearts and use it as a guide in their work and life, this will surely enrich and develop their beliefs as well. There are many kinds of human beliefs. There are 7 billion people in the world. There is no denying that there are 7 billion beliefs. This is because human beings are unique, even though they live under the same social and cultural values. For example, in addition to religious, philosophical, and scientific beliefs, life experience is the basis of another major belief.

They are renewed and changed at every stage of human life. Even the country of residence changes when you move. It can be said that belief is the core of a person's worldview. Some people are easily swayed by unproven evidence. For example, they believe in things that can be seen, that there is magical power, and so on. But all of them are things that we don't fully understand, that are just speculations that we perceive through emotions and fears, and information about them. I don't believe in that. This is because there is a scientific way to gain knowledge that is convincing and proven to be true. Knowledge gained in this way is considered to have a high probability of being true. An example of the knowledge gained in this way is the concept of solar energy. Solar energy is the energy that creates, sustains and nourishes all the processes on our planet. This has been proven thousands of times by scientific experiments, observations, measurements and analysis. The system of knowledge about the effects of the sun on our planet and the interaction of energy with other planets has become a theory. The theory is that some people think of tens of pages or volumes of books. But that is not the case. It can be expressed in a few lines. For example, a formula can be called a theory. Similarly, scientific articles, historical books, political analysis, personal biographies, etc., are all manifestations of a person's beliefs. By reading and studying these, it is understandable that other people - readers - also develop, correct, change and enrich their own beliefs.

Literature also preserves the author's beliefs in the image. People are constantly on the lookout for new ways to change and improve their beliefs. Beliefs are something that changes. What exactly do you believe in? What are your beliefs? If you ask someone, they will be surprised. What are you talking about? The answer is that in today's age of information and knowledge, anyone and anything can be trusted. You can trust anything. It's also a time for beliefs. You can trust God, you can trust Demons. Imagine that there is a sect-community of believers in the deer and the devil. Of course, it would be inexhaustible to enumerate the forms and types of beliefs that some people believe in, such as belief in aliens and scientific knowledge.

Beliefs can be divided into religion, philosophy, science and non-science, as well as pseudo science, mythology and superstition. Some see beliefs as experiences.

Life experience is the foundation of human beliefs. For example, a Mongolian herder or nomad does not sit in his tipi – called ger full of books and study them. Instead, by observing and experiencing the state of nature, human and animal life, one creates a very personal and self-confident belief. It is more a life experience than a religious or philosophical one. Beliefs are constantly changing, depending on where the person lives and the channels through which they acquire knowledge

Beliefs are constantly changing and evolving as knowledge is accumulated through channels. Also, some people update their mental "software" beliefs with new information and knowledge, as if they are constantly updating their computer Windows software, and if necessary, they give up their previous views, worldviews, and beliefs. Growing up in a communist-socialist regime, we have always believed in the victory of that social system. However, when the system became stagnant, we realised that there could be a different alternative, a different system, and in the struggled to find a way to create it, Mongols accepted the ideology of liberal beliefs against socialism and communism without hesitation. But now life has shown that even liberal ideas are not the right worldviews. This is just a political ideology. Understandably, a person's beliefs change. As a child, I believed in a fairy-tale world and later dropped out of school as a result of culture. Scientific knowledge, religion, and philosophy will replace it.

He will first receive it after comparing it with his own life experience and other knowledge and experience he has. We also listen to the opinions and criticisms of others. Then you can use that knowledge and information to make your own decisions. It should be done. A person's beliefs play a vital role in accepting reality, responding to the situation, looking to the future, and selling the consequences of what they are doing.

Our beliefs are a pillar of our self-confidence, anticipating and interpreting the process, creating something new, being inspired by it, finding a positive sense of optimism. Everyone knows that belief is very important in being human. But it's also interesting how and where we get our beliefs. Our beliefs are the creation and "interpretation" of our minds. Some people's beliefs have already been established, stabilized, and influenced by thousands of religions and philosophies. Some are formed through the experimental effects of ancestral life and their use in life. Some people believe in the knowledge gained through the sixth sense. They say it has been proved by mathematical modelling. When a person talks about his or her beliefs, he or she talks about what role he or her belief has played in his or her life. It is often said that the knowledge gained through that sixth sense changed our lives. Modern science, however, explains that the sixth sense is human intuition. Man not only knows the world by logical means but also intuitively. In these intuitions, the knowledge gained in the process of learning must be logically translated. In this way, human knowledge and beliefs are renewed and enriched. While scientists prefer to be causal and logical, there are times when the assumptions and explanations of what they are studying seem to be true. As a result of this perception, new truths and ideas have emerged that make theories, doctrines, and dogmas that were previously considered immutable truths "ruins." New ideas for individuals, society and humanities are born. There have been new truths and new ideas for doing. In many cases, a new idea has the potential to changes the lives of individuals, societies and human beings. In most cases, we create our intellectual world. In doing so, any knowledge is created by examining it with one's own life, comparing it with one's own experience, or arguing, debating, testing, and proving the opposite. This is called logical cognition. On top of that idea, religion, people of science, specializes. The advice of knowledgeable people or experts is also important. The path to change and develop your beliefs and create your spiritual world is not an easy one.

But everyone tries to understand and interpret the world as accurately as possible. The knowledge that mankind has accumulated over thousands of years is like a net. They are somehow connected and intertwined. One node is considered to be a stable branch of knowledge, and the other is necessarily connected. It means they affect each other. By bubbling up this connection, one creates one's system of beliefs and views. Some people also have unsystematic beliefs. This type of belief is also an overly simplistic summary and a collection of scattered knowledge. There is a view that reality and the universe are systems. Then there will be a logical consequence and requirement that our knowledge and beliefs about it should be systematic. Reality is constantly evolving. Naturally, the language is constantly enriched with new words - terms. There are also many subtle things, such as words that exist in some nations, words that do not exist in other nations, words that do not exist at other times, and words that exist at other times.

For example, in the 16th century, there was no such thing as a computer. We recognize our perceptions of reality by putting them into words, explaining them, or replacing them with similar models and experiments. We also strive to know the ultimate truth. Absolute truth includes our firm views that we do not want to change. The knowledge that we never want to give up on is my ultimate belief - the truth. For example, God created the world. Truth is power. Faith-based on truth is also power! People gain faith in different ways. Some believe that it does not have to be a science-based belief that uses scientific tools. Physicists have found both theoretically and experimentally, that the universe is made up entirely of electrons and quarks, and that they are "empty" in the form of frequencies and waves. But for 4,000 years, Buddhists have been discussing emptiness. For example, beliefs between science and religion intersect. However, some religions also claim that their beliefs are inviolable, unchangeable, and indisputable. By rejecting such a thing, science is closer to everyday life. The human mind and brain are very similar to computers as I said above. Any computer comes with a Windows operating system. There is also a human gene program compared to humans. A person buys a computer, installs new software for his office, and removes unused software. When society accepts a new person, it is first programmed within the family, then at school, and then at work, and it is "programmed" to "program" different beliefs, customs, and ideas. Compared to a computer, a person can control himself and make choices, so he takes what he installs and throws it away, and builds his worldview and belief codes. The program of a society or a nation is constantly changing, and so is the person's program. It's like the process of changing and updating information on a computer's hard drive. It can be said that as a person becomes spiritually rich and developed, he or she will have a powerful program to overcome all kinds of difficulties and obstacles in life. Not just individuals. Nations too. Mankind. Today, the parallel world of the human mind has become the "Internet." This network is being used as a reprogramming network of the human brain. Man himself has become an integral part of this network. As we become part of the computer system, we become more and more like him. The renewal of the spiritual world, the development and expansion of new programs and information, is like a computer ... It means that the power of information technology makes it possible to install any belief program without even knowing it. That's why we should install our national program! People are looking for people who share their beliefs. That is why I want to share with you my views and beliefs about Eternal Heaven – Munkh Tengri. This belief of mine originated in the most powerful period of Mongolian history, and some programs and codes can be forgotten and later erased by computers under the influence of others. I'm not writing this book for academics, so it is not a history and its analysis.

Since it is intended for the general public, historical and scientific terms and expressions should not be used as much as possible.

Eternal Heaven (Munkh Tengri) – The Creative Universe!

There is no God, but the Creative Universe. It is Eternal Heaven – Munkh Tengri! This Eternal Heaven is visible and invisible light. The real Reality. Existence! The power of the Eternal Heaven is the flow of this visible and invisible light. This current of motion is the law of the creativity of the universe. To worship the Eternal Heaven is to worship the above light - the Light (Energy)! Whether we like it or not, we worship energy! "Under the Power of the Eternal Heaven - Tengri means to live under the power of the Creator, the sustainer, the creative and destructive energy of life. Life is the result and manifestation of the creative nature (motion) of Eternal Heaven's Force. This law of creativity is always a process of overcoming. Therefore, it is clear that we have to overcome, develop and change ourselves throughout our lives. Such a life is a moral and right life. A person who chooses the right path of life is creative. A person who has the opposite of a creative person is a victim of life. It means to worship the Eternal Heaven, to live under the power of the Eternal Heaven, and to live the will of the Eternal Heaven. A person who has nothing to worship is not a human being. To worship the Eternal Heaven means to live in tune with the great Creative Universe, in the tens of thousands of manifestations of nature. It means living under the power of Eternal Heaven. Why live? It means living the will of Eternal Heaven. This is a creative principle of life. Life is living with courage. This is a creative principle of life.

Life is a process of overcoming. Overcoming means overcoming oneself, one's weakness, ignorance (the enemy), and overcoming all obstacles to change.

Finding the power of Eternal Heaven does not mean finding the power of magic or supernatural. The power of the Eternal Heaven is the power that is "found" in us through the air we breathe, the food we eat and drink, and the power of nature. When the energy in our bodies is renewed by the power of the Eternal Heaven, we can be healthy, energetic, creative, free, and happy. As long as our lives are right and healthy, we blessed by the power of Eternal Heaven, and the power of Eternal Heaven will bless each of us! I would like to greet you. It is a blessing to each other for energy, freedom and happiness. All things in the universe are subject to the will of the Eternal Heaven, exist, and are renewed. The Eternal Heaven, or Universe, is a living ocean of infinite, great energy. This flow of energy is called the power of the Eternal Heaven. I like to say that the Universe - Eternal Heaven is Creative. The power of the Eternal Heaven is the "ocean" of energy for all things. This ocean of energy is always rippling, moving, exploding, pounding. This ocean is a world of energy that cannot be measured in time or space. We are one of those creations.

The process of birth, life, and death is the result of Eternal Heaven's motion and movement. Man is the highest creation of the Eternal Heaven. Therefore, man "comes" with the essence of the creative nature of the universe. Human creativity is manifested in the creation of new knowledge, information and values through a combination of different information - knowledge and ideas. For now, it is religion, philosophy, science, technology, morality, and so on. Art is the greatest one. Eternal Heaven is a living, united Being. There is nothing good or bad about him. Talking about good and bad is just our reaction to various phenomena and events in our reality. Therefore, the concept of good and bad is constantly changing and has a relative character. Everything can change, be renewed, transformed, and evolved. We are just one cell of this great, unified thing. It is impossible to separate oneself from him, to separate oneself from the world around him. Because mergers have an intrinsic nature of disintegration, confiscation, creation, good and bad, and even change of place.

As I said before, Eternal Heaven is an "ocean of energy." The Eternal Heaven is the eternal being that created us, the transcendent being, and the embodiment of our spiritual nature.

We are the embodiment of such a united force. It's just one of the thousands of substances and thousands of processes that vary in frequency and frequency after. We can evolve and change by processing or interacting with other energies. Death is a transformation of tens of thousands of entities of the world. There is nothing in this universe but energy. The universe itself is an ocean of energy; the universe itself is Eternal Heaven. Everything in the universe is information that we know and do not know - a combination of energy. We are also energy, an energy that thinks, move, grow old, work, get sick, swell, go pity, and love.

The Mongols used to talk about solving the riddle of the wheel of the universe. This means that if you know the Eternal Heaven, you know yourself, and the Eternal Heaven is also understood as the conscious side of reality, in other words, the subjective side. If we limit our vision of the whole world, we will not see movement, change, evolution, or development. Because energy is a real reality, everything can move and change. The matter is not a reality. It is the other side is of energy. The transformation of matter into energy, the transformation of energy into matter, is another law of the Eternal Heaven. Let's not forget that the Eternal Heaven is an ocean of energy. The power of the Eternal Heaven is the creative capacity of this sea. This energy is infinite. The manifestation of this creativity is the movement, evolution, interaction, balance, unity, disintegration, change, and transformation of all things in the universe. This ocean revolves, swirls, boils, changes forever, moves, transforms and surrounds (the universe).

His movements create new phenomena and individuality every moment, and he strives for order amid chaos. Since the Eternal Heaven has great power to create living things, we can also understand it to be alive. Mongolians have known and lived for a long time that Munkh Tenger is the father. Since he is alive and carries life, he will of course have the will. The driving force of man is his will. So what is the will of Eternal Heaven? The question arises. The will of the Eternal Heaven is his creativity. You have to break something into it to create something new.

The fact that nature is destroying everywhere and creating new life and new phenomena can be considered as a manifestation of the Creator's wills that is The Eternal Heaven. Eternal Heaven is the creative master of this universe. The beautiful words, "The universe is my religion, Nature is my church," can be seen and felt everywhere. To worship the Eternal Heaven is to worship the Life-bearing Universe. The Power of Eternal Heaven is essentially the life force that sustains and sustains all living things. It is from this power that all living things begin and is absorbed. What are reality and existence? is one of the questions that philosophy must answer. So my answer to this question is that Eternal Heaven is the only, eternal reality. Eternal Heaven is a living, creative, life-giving, life-sustaining, infinite universe that cannot be measured in space or time. The word universe – "orchlon" seems to come from the word "orchikh". Mongolian word "orchih" means moving, changing, transforming, evolving. The manifestation of this movement of the universe is its creativity. The universe, or Eternal Heaven, constantly "creates" living and non-living things in a certain form as it moves and swirls.

At the atomic, molecular, and electronic levels, they are under the influence of the Eternal Heaven's Force, or cosmic energy, and derive their energy from it. The power of the Eternal Heaven is the information-energy field of the Universe. The concept of "field" can be said to be the state of the quantum at the energy level. At this level, human consciousness and Eternal Heaven are one. In addition to unity, we can imagine that we create and change each other. Eternal Heaven is a philosophical concept. It is a category that represents all living things and the universe that carries the power of life. I call the Eternal Heaven the Universe. We think of the universe as lifeless planets, burnt suns, stars, cosmic gases, particles, meteorites, meteorite collisions, and chemical and hot nuclear reactions. So where did all living things come from? Where in the universe can the source, the source, the sponsor, the sponsor of life be? The source of all this is the power of Eternal Heaven! The power of the Eternal Heaven is the cosmic energy that creates and sustains all living and non-living things. It is only through this energy that we need to learn to understand and feel that life is flourishing, evolving, and gaining more and more power! The Eternal Sky is an infinite number of stars, galaxies, suns, moons, and planets that astronomers study. Of course, infinite things include innumerable finite events, phenomena, animals, plants, and intelligent beings.

- The Power of the Eternal Heaven -
The Creative Energy of the Universe.

Any substance is made up of molecules, atoms, electrons, neutrons, protons, quarks and so on. Everything in the universe is a complex of frequencies, flows, movements, and combinations of these particles. It is the flow of light, waves, and energy. This flow of energy is the power of the Eternal Heaven or the Cosmic Energy of the Universe! As mentioned in the previous chapter, the Eternal Heaven is an infinite space, a flow of energy that moves, transforms and changes forever in time. The Power of the Eternal Heaven is the flow of energy that creates and destroys the things of the Universe. This flow of energy is invisible to our eyes and invisible to our hands. According to the latest scientific research, 95% of the universe is invisible to us. Energy never dies, nor does it increase, subtract, or disappear. All living things in the world are linked by this energy level, and they are in the ocean of this energy and "dissolve" back into the ocean of energy. There is no such thing as a perishable phenomenon, but they merge.

The power of the Eternal Heaven, or universal cosmic energy, is the creative energy that creates, sustains, and "destroys" life. Eternal Heaven itself is an ocean of energy. One of the cells of this ocean, the "drop," the tiny individual, can be thought of as a human being. Man is the creation of the Eternal Heaven, the only thing that is nourished by the power of the Eternal Heaven. This is the energy that surrounds a person that drives him and sustains him. Metabolism is the basis of living organisms.

Metabolism is the exchange of energy. We are energy converters. The power of the Eternal Heaven is the energy that comes to us through nature. We replenish our energy by consuming, transforming, modifying, and consuming natural substances in our food. That is why we believe that Mother is the one who nourishes and nurtures - Nature. From breast milk, minerals and resources are all-natural energy. We are energy...energy that to walk, move, and think ... This quality is considered to be human and soul. We were energized before we were born, and after we were born, we were always after energy, and eventually, we became energy. In other words, it is reunited with the power of the Eternal Heaven. The universe is an ocean of energy! The power of Eternal Heaven is a creative force! Everything that happens in the universe, from birth to death and extinction, is the result of this creative transformation and movement of energy. The power of the eternal sky is a great power that creates, sustains and destroys life - energy! The Eternal Power of Heaven is the living force, the creator, sustainer, carrier, and creative force of life. The power of nature is simply the power of the Eternal Heaven. The power of the Eternal Heaven is a great force that moves, carries, and creates the lives of all beings: the Universe, Nature, Man, Society, Individuals, Animals, and Plants.

They are the power of nature, the power of humanity, the power of society and nation, the power of the individual, the power of consciousness and spirit.

The only force that carries and sustains the power of nature, the power of humanity, the power of society and nation, the power of the individual, the power of consciousness and spiritual power is the power of the Eternal Heaven. All these forces can be considered as different manifestations of the one and only Eternal Heaven's Power. We need to learn to see and feel that great power in everything, in every stone, in every leaf and flower. The power of Eternal Heaven is a great force that sustains, sustains, and creates life! It's like radio waves, electromagnetic waves. It is on this wave that all things in the universe work, connect, harmonize, move, change, evolve, and transform in order. If one loses contact with this flow of energy, one will be held hostage by the so-called material things around him and will be confined to a limited life. That means we can't be limited to the five senses. There may be a sixth or even a seventh sense behind it! Such levels of sensation have been debated for millennia. If the flow of the power of the Eternal Heaven is the driving force of the life of the universe, then the source and driving force behind the life of any human being is also this great force. The essence of the worship of power is that Mongolians worship this divine power of ours. We seem to "forget" that we are connected to this great power because of our daily commotion, our busy schedule, and our busy lives. Eternal Heaven, the infinite, eternal thing beyond the limits of the universe that we have yet to know and "see." This Eternal Heaven is made up of tens and thousands of universes. The power that connects, animates moves, creates, and "destroys" these universes is the Power of the Eternal Heaven!

The power of the Eternal Heaven is the main force of life. It can be said to be the soul of everything. It is a reality carrier. This includes the flow of our minds. So this life-sustaining flow is the flow of the power of the Eternal Heaven! This energy will flow to us through all of nature and all living things. The power of the Eternal Heaven is a powerful wave of energy and its flow that creates all phenomena under the control of space and time. A stream that flows through everything. Thanks to the power of the Eternal Heaven, all things live, flourish, move, evolve, and transform. They follow their path of evolution and join the great current. Of course, nothing can exist without the power of Eternal Heaven. This begs the question. Eternal Heaven is considered the Universe. So why not just call it the Universe, the power of the Eternal Heaven is called cosmic energy? The question is. Why Eternal Heaven or the Power of Eternal Heaven? Here we are talking about Divine Quality. Of course, the concepts of the universe and cosmic energy are scientific. More specifically, astrophysics is a term used in astronomy. Science treats things independently of the researcher, realistically and objectively. In other words, the researcher and the subject are separate. Then there is no such thing in the universe, and we are an integral part of the ocean of energy. We have no choice but to connect this ability to consider it as a whole with our spiritual-divine nature. When you look at it like that, the so-called Eternal Heaven, the Eternal Heaven's Power, looks like a spiritual and divine thing. In this sense, the so-called power of Heaven and Eternal Heaven seems to be a spiritual and divine thing. In this sense, they are living beings, living energy. All forms of life and all power come from Him alone! Lightning, the ropes of the oceans, the impulses, the coincidences of the sun and the moon, and everything that changes in motion is manifestations and results of this great force! The "breath" of Eternal Heaven is the power of Eternal Heaven. From the light of Andromeda to the flame of a lamp in the temple, everything is a manifestation of this great energy! This is the power of Eternal

Heaven! The gravity of the world, the flow of our thoughts, the love of man, are all an integral part of this power, its manifestation. It's called energy in the physical sciences, but because it's a philosophical concept of our Mind, we should call it the Power of Eternal Heaven! This power is present in everything, like electromagnetic waves, and it is invisible to the naked eye, just like the air that sustains life, and there is no limit. The immeasurable energy of the Sun, Moon, Earth, and stars, which is a combination of all kinds of energy, is nothing more than a manifestation of the Power of the Eternal Heaven. The colour combination of all the things and phenomena in the universe is this light - the flow, the manifestation, the combination of light! Only by the power of the Eternal Heaven are the things of the universe in eternal circulation. A rose petal cannot bloom without this power, and a newborn child's smile or cry is a manifestation of this power. This light can be understood by Mongolians as the love of Heaven - Father, who gives us real energy, freedom and happiness. There is also a lack of verbal power to put all this into words. This light is the stream of the life force - the power of the Eternal Heaven! The Power of Eternal Heaven is a stream of visible and invisible light!

- The Law of Eternal Heaven - The Law of Creativity

When you say "will", you are talking about something conscious and spiritual?!

You may remember that in previous chapters, Eternal Heaven was a field of information and energy. The field of information and the field of energy are inseparable. The mind of the Eternal Heaven is the realm of that information. The power of the Eternal Heaven is cosmic energy and the quantum field. Of course, everything conscious is motivated. That willpower is always creative and inclined. The law of eternal heaven is the principle of his self-transformation. This is an eternal and unique principle. It is the origin, purpose, meaning, and cause of life. Life is a fluctuation of the power of the Eternal Tengri. Man has all the power, all the information, all the energy of the Universe, and he has to use it to realize the creativity of the universe. The law of Eternal Heaven is the will of Eternal Heaven. That is why we live and understand Eternal Heaven as Heavenly Father. Eternal Heaven is a whole, made up of tens of thousands of sounds. The movement, development, transformation of the world, the cause of evolution, and the driving force is the power of the Eternal Heaven! What pervades the universe is the field of information and energy. This field is the creator of all species and all living beings. "

What pervades the universe is the field of information and energy. This country is a "producer" of all things and all living things. Exactly how it is produced, by vibrations and frequencies! Science has established that the basis for the solid, liquid, gaseous, and plasma states of phenomena is the energy (atomic molecule) frequencies that make them up. In other words, the harder the whole, the slower the vibrations. However, the volatile and gaseous state means that there is a lot of variabilities. At the level of this information field, everything is interconnected and networked as one. This one thing - Eternal Heaven! So Eternal Heaven is one thing. Although we experience and experience tens of thousands of things and all beings in our daily lives through our five senses, they are all manifestations of one thing. Everything in the world is a manifestation of information, energy and matter. Everything is a manifestation of these three things.

Creativity is the nature of denying and dismissing the old for something new to exist. I want Mongolia to develop with this law of creativity. We Mongolians have always valued and respected human creativity and natural creativity. The law of creativity is the universal law of the universe! It is the nature of the world for all new things to replace the old. A changeable person is a creative person who consciously or unknowingly applies this principle. One has to change oneself, one's room, one's world. Creativity begins with breaking and changing. This is the nature of the universe. Creativity begins with breaking and changing. If we translate this state of the universe into human action, we will know ourselves in the process of recognizing the universe, and we will also change ourselves as we renew and change our surroundings. The process of overcoming one's stagnation is the manifestation and realization of one's creativity. The most stagnant people are missionaries, monks, and people who have been brainwashed by some political or religious ideology. They are the ones who try to preserve their religion and ideology and live as prisoners within the framework of what they are used to. They are so used to it that they don't dare to change or create it. They fight to the death to maintain that status, and they also spread the ideology of justifying themselves as if they were fighting for "justice - a good thing." In this way, they "fight" in groups and become a real stagnant mass. It has become their rule that they become so numerous that they vehemently oppose any change or reform. Such an attempt to take away and save the old order, morality, ideology, and way of life is in itself against the Law of Eternal Heaven. In this way, individuals and societies fall into an unhealthy path. Only a healthy society and individual can change and innovate! Calling themselves "honest - good people" and fighting to protect the old is the only way to see human society as an animal. It is the denial of creative talent and the divine spirit of man, and the protection of an average, inactive, sluggish life. It is from this state that the individual protects a sedentary, sluggish life. This is the only way to stagnate, both personally and socially. The enemy of a herd of "fair-good" people is always the creative individual. We, Mongolians, need to understand that this is the highest aspiration of humankind and any country, the main principle of human development - the manifestation of the law of Eternal Heaven. The individual who finds change, innovation, and creativity overcomes the hardships of life and invites the power of light - the power of Eternal Heaven - to Earth. Therefore, it can be said that a creative person suffers a lot. It is a normal and common phenomenon to turn into the joy of life because it is a suffering for self-transformation and renewal!

The Meaning of the slogan "Under the Power of Eternal Heaven ...!"

Under the Power of Eternal Tengri or Heaven means the will to gain power. That is why the ultimate goal is to find the power of Eternal Heaven. To attain the power of Eternal Heaven is to attain enlightenment. Everyone wants strength, freedom and happiness. Eternal Heavenly Power is the foundation and source of true power, freedom, and happiness. This can be a basic condition for the development and strength of any society. To live under the power of Eternal Heaven means to worship and live in this great power. To worship the forces of the Eternal Heavens is to worship the forces of the Universe and Nature. This is the basis of the spiritual approach to nature. The power of the universe is nothing more than cosmic information – the energy field. The – waves of electricity. The field of force - nothing more than a wave. Everything in the universe is under the power of the Eternal Heaven. This principle of existence has been known to the Mongols for a long time, and it is based on this principle that Chinggis Khan the Great conqueror of the World.

Chinggis Khan's "philosophy" was "Under the Power of the Eternal Heaven ..." It may be in this one sentence ... The driving force that sustains life's energy. The Power of Eternal Heaven! This is the only power beyond all will, sin, virtue, and all that is happening in the universe. It can be said that the whole life of Chinggis Khan was a manifestation and implementation of this principle. Life itself is a manifestation of the power and movement of the Eternal Heaven, and in the language of modern science, it is vibration. Man's will is also a manifestation of the power of the Eternal Heaven, without which nothing can be changed, stimulated, exalted, or prospered. This philosophy of Chinggis Khan's life should be a philosophy of our life – our struggle. The principle -"Under the power of Eternal Heaven ...! "- should be the philosophy of life, worldview, the purpose of life, meaning, the driving force of history, the starting point of Mongolian morality. In short, it is the only driving force of existence, the pole of truth, the supreme principle of life! Life is a struggle. This struggle requires infinite power, and that energy is the Power of the Eternal Heaven! That is why our ancestors rode their horses, praying, "Under the power of the Eternal Heaven ...!" That is why they were able to unite the world under one banner. The banner of the Eternal Heaven is the banner of the principle that the power of the body, the mind, and the spirit prevails under the rule of the truth.

The main principle of this law of nature is that under the Force of Eternal Heaven, the banner of the implementation of the principle that the power of the mind and intellect prevails. The concept of the power of the Eternal Heaven is a category of philosophy. This includes not only the forces of nature and energy, but also the forces of the human body, mind, intellect, moral principles, politics, economics, and ideology. That is why the Mongol soldiers of the Empire had the idea that their physical, mental and spiritual strength comes from the power of the Eternal Heaven. It seems that being under the power of the Eternal Heavens not only expressed a desire for power, but also a person's physical, mental, and spiritual condition. It is in this state that one must find the strength to overcome and overcome anything. Throughout history, Mongolians have faced three challenges. We are people who worship nature and are close to nature. One of the three things is to overcome the persecution and ignorance of foreign religions, the second is to develop one's body, mind, and spirit, to eradicate greed and falsehood, to be faithful to one's master, and to have a deep understanding of one's duty to humanity. We conclude that the worst of the world would have been to overcome the ugliness, the cowardice, the treachery, the cruelty. In this way, the yellow pages of history have proved that he ruled the world, established the principle of nature as human beings, human beings as companions, and the principle that war should never be waged for evil purposes.

Researchers have focused on the secret of Chinggis Khan's power. They paid a lot of attention to what it was. In particular, there is a great deal of controversy about the worship of the emperor's claim Sacred Mountain Burkhan Khaldun on the ascent of the Eternal Heaven's Power. Everyone concluded that the concept of Eternal Heaven and the power of Eternal Heaven was his vision and belief in the universe. That was his philosophy of life ... From an early age; he realized that life was not just a small success, but a struggle for energy, victory and freedom. No one would argue that he was able to train and guide soldiers and generals who were as strong as iron, as light, as liquids, and as strong as walls.

Under the power of Eternal Heaven ...! The principle was the golden rule that permeated everything in the life of the Empire.

Any war is fought by queens who are tolerant of other people's religions, who have overcome them, who have created an army that is in high demand and intolerant of any weakness, and who have nurtured courage, heroism, and unwavering courage to win the battle.

Under the power of the Eternal Heaven to fight and conquer the world…! It can be said that the word was a prayer, a recitation, an encouragement to victory. "Under the power of Eternal Heaven …! "Should not be taken lightly. It is not the notion of oppressing others by physical force, material power, weapon power, magical power, or celestial power, which is to blame the weak before the mighty. This is not a materialistic conception of power. It is a matter of creativity, and it must be understood in the sense that the power of the Eternal Heaven is always a new, creative force in the universe. If we live under the power of Eternal Heaven, it should be understood as the creative force of the universe. We need to understand that we will be liberated if we live under the power of Eternal Heaven. Why be free? To create! To create, we must live in constant connection with the great power, the immeasurable power. Life contains eternal creativity. Therefore, the idea is that if we live under the power of the Eternal Heaven, we will never be stagnant or backward. Without this power, we will be overwhelmed and weakened in our ability to control our lives. Life takes place under the power of the Eternal Heaven and flourishes. The power of the Eternal Heaven is the driving force behind all the changes, innovations and evolutions that take place in the individual, society and the universe. During the reign of the Emperor, life was a battleground for the Mongols. Suppressing the invading enemy opened up new possibilities for them, and they continued to conquer. Life change and competition, but stopping, sitting, and indulging were the beginning of the catastrophes. It can be said that the Great Khan saw the decay of settled civilizations. It can be said that he healed, healed and mobilized these vile, selfish and stagnant societies. He saw for the first time that as they became disconnected from nature and life, they became societies of greed, slavery, and unjust aggression. Defeated civilizations did not realize his great purpose! It can be said that defeated civilizations have written about him as a savage, rude, and immoral terrorist because they did not realize this great goal. However, they have flattened many cities and civilizations, and in their place have emerged better and healthier civilizations. Christianity came to a standstill and brought a living morality and a new ethic that connected Heaven and Earth to the extreme civilizations of weakness. In obedient and mortal societies, they opened the way to a new way of life, under the power of the Eternal Heaven. We need to understand that this is not a destructive force, but a great force for rebirth. This is what the Great Khan bequeathed to us by his deeds. Under the power of Eternal Heaven...!

- Munkh Tengerism and the Science

We have come here to say that Eternal Heaven is the Universe. It would be useful to clarify what modern science considers the universe to be. Modern science divides the universe into two categories: macro (large) and micro (small). The macro-universe includes the stars, the sun, the moon, and distant galaxies, ranging from visible and tangible phenomena to modern astronomical telescopes. The microcosm is a world in which molecules, atoms, electrons, protons, neutrons, neutrinos, photons, and quarks become smaller and smaller and turns into electro-magnetic waves. But these two worlds are two sides of the same coin, creating and forming each other. Interestingly, when viewed at this micro level, the universe is whole and infinite. This whole universe is understood as an ocean of infinite energy. It is an ocean of light and energy that we can understand as the Eternal Heaven.

What is the Universe or Eternal Heaven? We think of galaxies, planets, planets, and moons, measured in billions of light-years. The light-year is the distance light travels in one year. Everyone knows that light travels 300,000 kilometres per second. Then it is clear what kind of space a billion light-years will be. Let's put aside our talk of this giant space and giant bodies and go back to the microcosm. The process of the microcosm, on the other hand, takes place in space, about 1 mm and 1 second divided by billions of times. It's impossible to know what's going on there! This is because the particles are constantly moving in two states, only in the form of waves, the frequencies of which can be determined. This is what some physicists call "emptiness" and is synonymous with the emptiness of Buddhism. According to modern science (physics), the universe around us is made up of atoms, atoms that are invisible to the naked eyes, such as protons, neutrons, electrons, and neutrinos. So far, there are 12 such types of particles. Protons and neutrons make up the nucleus of an atom, while neutrons are made up of particles called quarks. The whole universe is made up of something called a particle wave. There is an electron. We use a variety of appliances. They work on the principle of using electronic flow.

There are also various streams of light, including sunlight, which is a stream of particles called photons. There is a quantum theory of light, which explains what a small part of an atom is, or a light wave. In the quantum state, things are imagined as waves. This wave will cover the whole universe. In other words, if a quantum is understood as a particle, it can exist in different spaces at the same time. It can be compared to a mirror. Suppose you put 100 mirrors facing each other and stand in the middle. Your image will appear to be infinite. And when you move your hand, those figures of yours move at the same time without any mistakes. Of course, it would be a mistake to try to move people into different rooms. Physicists have determined that the quanta in different space and time environments are the same. Experiments have shown that such small particles also interact with each other regardless of space. This is called quantum entanglement, mixing, and combination. In English, this is called the "quantum state". We are also made up of atoms, molecules, and electrons. It is easy to imagine that even these small particles are subject to this general law of the universe. We know that atomic molecules are millions of times smaller. Then time will pass there millions of times faster. We learned in high school that there was a small particle around the atom called an electron. However, physicists have tried to determine its location, but so far have failed. Instead, our current technologies work by determining that they can flow, stop, and measure in a certain direction based on their charge.

By determining that it is possible to measure, our current electrical appliances are working. It also combines protons, neutrons and electrons to create more than 100 elements. Everything in the world is created only by the appropriate and unique combinations of these three. In other words, the formula is Proton + Neutron + Electron = Universe. Light is a stream of particles called photons! Sunlight is the flow of this photon. This light is the cosmic energy we feel the most. The power of Eternal Tengri! Why is it that this phenomenon of the universe, which is made up of scattered, high-velocity protons, neutrons, and electrons, finds a stable form that does not disperse, separate, or dissolve? The question arises. Then there is another particle that holds these particles in place, and it's called the meson. For now, this is just a riddle, and it is impossible to say for sure that it exists until it is confirmed experimentally. We can talk about many more particles in the future, but I will end this here because it is not intended to be a textbook of physics or to explain the quantum theory. So far, there are 6 scientifically proven particles and a total of 12. These are hypothetical particles. There are three great forces between the particles in the universe. They are:

- Strong interactions: Atoms do not split. Tied state of particles.

- Weak Interactions: A thermo nuclear reaction that causes the loss or unties of particles.

- Electromagnetic interactions: Solar photon flux, Earth's magnetic field, etc.

In addition to these forces, some scientists add a fourth force, which is the force of gravitational interaction. This force is currently only in the experimental and research phase, and these three forces have been confirmed by experimental observations. The stronger the interaction, the slower the ability of the particles to overcome that force. At this point, a mass of matter is formed. Mass, on the other hand, depends on the vibration and the intensity with which the particles interact. If we consider the interaction and flow of particles as energy, then the delay of this state that depends on it can be considered as mass. Thus Einstein's formula was written. Energy is a simple formula that is equal to the mass multiplied by the square of the speed of light. The action of these forces is considered to be fluctuations. In general, it can be said that particles exist and move in the same way as oscillations and radio waves. Thus we can imagine that nature and the universe are made up of several layers or dimensions. Things are made up of atoms. The atom has a nucleus, and the nucleus is made up of protons, neutrons, and electrons. At this level, everything in the universe transforms into waves, allowing us to imagine an eternal and infinite ocean of energy, the Eternal Heaven. From this, we can conclude that the Eternal Heaven is the ocean of energy, and the Eternal Heaven's power is the flow of light and energy - current. Now, what is the human mind?

If there is a universal law that all things in the universe interact and move with each other, let's exchange a few words about how our minds affect the universe. The idea of how the human mind can connect and interact with Eternal Heaven. Many would say they can. Man can create and change a lot with the power of his mind. We are changing the Earth, sometimes destroying it, launching satellites into space, operating space stations, creating and using radio waves, the Internet, television, and so on. Of course, all this would be impossible without the quantum theory and practice of modern physics. At the beginning of the last century, physicists made experiments and made a discovery. It is called the Heisenberg Quantum Uncertainty Principle after the person who discovered the phenomenon. As a result of this experiment, the electrons were distributed in the same way as anyone who observes the flow of electrons would think. In other words, when an observer sees an electron being exposed to a small piece of a measuring instrument, the small particle "looks like" in the form of a particle, ceases to observe, and after a while looks again in the form of waves. This process was manifested in the way the observer imagined. What this means is that our thoughts are influencing reality or physical phenomena. We know that our brains and hearts emit electromagnetic waves and work on such waves. This can be confirmed by the fact that we have normal brain scans and magnetic heart scans that are used by every doctor. Our brain undergoes a very powerful biochemical reaction, and quanta radiate from our brains in all directions in the form of waves. Today, computers, prostheses, and various electrical devices can be controlled and operated by waves emitted from the human brain. It is one of the most common phenomena in life to experience a lot of souls when a person dies or is on the verge of clinical death. The brain is a supercomputer that stores all the sensations, knowledge, experiences, and information we experience throughout our lives. These are stored in the brain as quantum information. When we die, when we are taken out to the Universe - Eternal Heaven, we "see" a lot of information, like a movie. It is at this point that the ambiguous principle of the quantum state described above emerges, and the material universe and the mind and consciousness begin to merge. The brain does not produce anything material of its own accord but radiates energy that has been transformed into a definite, stable electric charge and electromagnetic form. This is what we call a soul-spirit. We know that the spirit is always understood, depicted, and imagined as light. In this way, all the good and bad experiences we have accumulated in our lives take the form of energy and are reunited with the Eternal Heaven, where the spirits of our ancestors are united. This is something that has been scientifically proven over the centuries - the process of life and death. Nothing goes anywhere! All the information written in our brains is in the form of an energy wave, and we can say that evolution is moving to a new stage of development. This, too, is scientifically based and is proved by the universal law of "the law of conservation of energy." The law" is proved by the universal law of eternity. Energy law states that information does not perish, but passes from one form to another, that we are only one form of energy, and that it does not perish, but evolves. It's as if that energy, that bright radiant spirit, is coming back to this material universe. It is not a lie to say that our souls are born into this universe by finding different bodies just to gain experience. This process makes us think about the spiritual soul, which is immortal. From all this, we can see that we are not separate from the things of the universe, but at the level of particles, atoms and electrons, we are a drop of the ocean, a unit of the Eternal Heaven. At this level, we can see from these experiments that our minds are affected by so-called real and material things and processes. Everything that can be imagined in our thoughts and minds can become reality. Thus we are alive, united with the Eternal Heaven as a whole, with the possibility of His eternal creative power!

- Munkh Tengerism - Mongolian Spiritual Philosophy

Mankind is entering its third millennium. They face many challenges. Among them are terrorism, local and national armed conflicts for ecological and natural resources, raw materials, food shortages, drugs, the corona virus, and the economic and electronic wars of the superpowers. The situation makes humanity think about how to survive. In such a situation, the need to have an orderly worldview, a place in society and nature, and a sense of responsibility to oneself and others is becoming more and more important. Philosophy plays an important role in the formation of a person's worldview. It is a philosophy that determines the meaning of any society, the values to be followed, and the means to achieve its goals. After the fall of the totalitarian regime, Mongolia has changed beyond recognition in the name of the so-called transition to "democracy". No one knows that the 21st century is beginning in a very critical and tragic way for Mongolia. To use a healthy ecological environment and vast natural resources for the benefit of our people, we need to analyze the situation from a philosophical point of view, find a reason and choose a way forward, plan and focus. Philosophy is most useful in times of social unrest, and the forefront of any change lies in the capacity of human philosophical thinking. The current situation requires modern Mongolians to have philosophical knowledge, and it is the culture of philosophical thinking that should become an integral part of the culture of our society. I think it is necessary to say here that philosophy is a science that reveals the secrets of nature, society and the nature of human life and teaches people how to live in harmony with nature and society. Philosophy is not just an abstract theoretical model and imagination, but a concept of the nature and morality of living life.

Worldview is one of the most important factors in human consciousness. Everyone develops a worldview in the course of their lives, and it is common for everyone to be unique - individual.

But everyone is a member of society. It is clear, then, that society exists because it has something in common with everyone's worldview. What exactly is a worldview? The question arises as to whether the content of an individual's view of the world changes and develops from generation to generation throughout the life and history of an individual or society. A worldview is, first and foremost, how an individual or a society perceives reality. In this understanding, of course, in addition to gaining a real knowledge of that reality, one acquires a value orientation in the process of applying that knowledge to one's life and well-being. In other words, the relationship between "man" and "the world" is formed as an interpretation of understanding. Philosophy is a system of generalized knowledge. The wider the scope of that knowledge, the more secure the individual, society, and nation will see the world, and the more stable it will be. Moreover, the worldview is not a summary of knowledge. It is systematic knowledge of the interdependence and interrelationships of man, society, and nature, and the ability to respond to the challenges of a given historical era.

How are we Mongolians philosophically today? - Do we have faith? Is there a belief that can make a united nation an integral part of an important spiritual quality? Beliefs are not just about thinking. It also includes emotional tendencies. Beliefs are a set of principles, views and ideas of one's own life. Is there such a thing in our society? - Do we have something called Spiritual Values? We have already traded our perceptions of good and bad, in maintaining a proper relationship between the individual and society. This value is nurtured throughout one's life. But do we have the conditions to develop and develop like that today? No more! The concept of value is not knowledge. Knowledge is the result of recognizing reality. Instead, it can be said that the attitude towards the environment with different interests, needs and desires is an orientation of society and human values. Then we are also losing that identity. Do we have the highest aspirations? It became the ultimate goal and the direction of development. Is there a supreme value that every member of society should look in that direction like a "Polar Star" and communicate and work together? No! We don't have a common goal that we all aspire to and value, except for the fact that everyone is whistling to get rich and be proud of their brand.

- Do we have a "religion" that is innate, native, and derived from our culture? Apart from Buddhism and its most backward form - Lamaism, we also have nothing to worship nowadays! National philosophy is a set of universal social principles, including norms, personal development trends, and moral norms that have been developed, preserved, and inherited throughout the history of a society. It's still missing! Do we have principles of life and work? Most of us don't have that either. It is a principle of responsibility and understanding of oneself and others, which one understands in terms of society and nature. Some standards and rules have been established throughout history. Some principles govern our activities according to the needs of our society. However, earning income without working and finding people with such principles in today's Mongolia, where officials have plundered public funds, is a difficult task. All of this is an integral and necessary part of the worldview of both individuals and societies. We now need to rebuild our worldview. It also requires knowledge, information, and a scientific basis that is accurate and proven. Of course, not everyone is a scientist. But we also have resources. We can grow our worldview out of life and practice. This is our philosophy of life, which has been preserved for a long time in the depths of our understanding, ideas and social consciousness of the Eternal Heaven. You can grow your worldview. This is our philosophy of life, which has been preserved for a long time in the depths of our understanding, ideas and social consciousness of the Eternal Heaven. This knowledge has been present in folklore, proverbs, parables, epics, shamanism, and their poetry since ancient times. There is no need to unnecessarily theorize, religiose, politicize, or propagate the philosophy of the Eternal Tengri. It is a philosophy of everyday life that does not need to be logically boxed, systematized, categorized, and is an inexhaustible part of the Mongolian nomad's culture that can continue to develop in this way. The practice of shamanism was the first stage of the philosophy of the Eternal Tengri. The mythical world of Mongolia is inextricably linked with shamanism, and the cult of the great forces of nature, the worldview, and morality are rooted in it. Not only in Mongolia but all over the world, shamanism has been tested and improved by various nations, which is a testament to the fact that this nature-worshipping theory, theory and practice has been tested by life and has yielded results. In the course of human development, various religions have emerged in connection with labour, society, the economy, the division of labour, and urbanization. At that time, religion was the dominant worldview, recognizing reality and applying it in practice. Religion is a world with many facets and many meanings. Even today, with the advancement of science and technology, religion is still a force to be reckoned with. Religion is not only a way of recognizing reality through the mind and emotions but also a way of understanding religious values and moral teachings.

In addition to being a means of identification through movement, religious values and moral teachings continue to form the highest aspirations of society and the individual. The values of religious love, good deeds, endurance, forgiveness, kindness, generosity, responsibility, and justice still meet the spiritual needs of millions today. It can be concluded that the idea of Eternal Tengri has already passed this religious stage and is on its way to becoming a philosophy. The philosophical worldview provides a general picture of the world. It is an explanation of the nature of existence or reality and the relationship between human lives.

The philosophy of the Eternal Heaven or Munkh Tengerism is the philosophy of life. It is a worldview that combines life experiences with the results of scientific cognition. This philosophy can provide complete answers to questions about knowledge, values, society, politics, ethics, and the arts. It can also provide an individual with basic guidelines on how to approach the world and how to manage one's work and life. While science studies reality in isolation and keeps the researcher free from reality, the philosophy of the Eternal Heavens studies man and reality through contemplation and cultivation. It is a way for an individual to recognize the outside world by approaching the inside. Philosophical culture is the criterion for expanding and recognizing one's spirituality. The main subjects of philosophy are Man and Nature. The philosophy of Eternal Heaven answers this as follows. Man and nature are inseparable. Materialism and idealism do not have to be polarized, and since all things are united, these two directions can be considered as two sides of the same thing. The question of man is the most important in the philosophy of Eternal Heaven. From the moment a person is born into this world, he continues to understand himself in isolation from the world. Our philosophical and cultural tradition says that man and the world are one.

Munkh Tengerism – Worshiping to the Nature

No society can exist without nature. It is a scientific fact that man came from nature. Nature is the basis of human existence. The difference between nature and man, the question of interaction and future trends, has become a pressing issue for today's humanity. Ever since man was discovered, he has sought to understand his surroundings and his position in them. For

Mongolians, nature and man were not seen as opposites and separate things. On the contrary, throughout history, it has been viewed as a single entity, one that cannot exist without nature. In Western society, however, with the development of science and technology, the scope of understanding and interacting with nature has increased, and there is a growing perception that nature is something that should be used to meet human needs. It can be said that Mongolians have always believed that the earth, water, animals, plants, the blue sky, the universe, and the Eternal Heaven are the sources that sustain their lives and should be loved and protected as their parents. What is nature for Mongolians?

For Mongolians, what nature means is, first of all, the Eternal Heaven - the Universe, the Mother Nature, everything that exists is a living thing. Then there are the places where they live, Mongolian nature, land, water, plants and animals. All of these are undoubtedly the source of food, air, and household consumption that sustains Mongolians. The fact that society is an integral part of nature and can survive on it is deeply ingrained in Mongolians' view of nature and society. Mongolians are well aware that the process of life can take place as long as they cannot survive without nature and are in constant contact with nature. As we have lived in the depths of nature for centuries, we have come to understand that man and nature have one thing in common. Despite this community connection, there is, of course, a difference between man and nature. The power of nature is a "blind" force, and it makes no sense to talk about good and bad here. In the case of human society, however, social power and law are different from nature, because every human action has a purpose and a conscious action. While natural laws and laws are eternal laws, human social laws are relatively short-lived. This is because human society changes very quickly compared to nature. It is not so difficult to understand the laws of nature, but it is quite difficult to understand the laws of society. Man can live in harmony with nature like any other animal but he can have a powerful influence on nature as he changes and adapts to his needs. Man's ability to find his own needs and to meet his ever-increasing needs is constantly evolving, and his impact on the environment is growing stronger and wider. Man-made, organized activities eventually turned man into something unnatural. Animals repair their nests by instinct and by the laws of nature, while humans consciously change natural phenomena by planning from the beginning. Another big human factor in society. It can be said that social cohesion changes nature. Man cannot exist without nature and society. Mankind today interacts with nature in three ways.

1. The use of natural resources in cash,

2. The use of natural resources for industrial and agricultural purposes,

3. The so-called noosphere - a rational activity that connects man and nature, technology, socio-political and economic life, urbanization, etc. creating an environment other than one's nature. The result of mankind's activities and its labour - vehicles, power plants, recreation areas, animals, plants, artificial lakes, rivers, canals, garbage, waste, polluted air, radioactive land and oceans.

The negative impact of human activities on the environment is expanding year by year and is on the verge of a crisis. Nature is not a human creation, but the source of life that creates nourishes and sustains man. Nature is necessary conditions for human existence, life and activity. All living things on the earth's surface are considered to be the biosphere, while the man-made environment is called the noosphere. The fact that the two are now at odds with each other is a tragedy of civilization. The reason for the stalemate is that the damage to the environment is directed against it. This requires a new approach to nature, a source of energy that is not harmful to the environment, and solutions for food and waste. To address this, humanity needs to make fundamental changes in its industrial, political, economic and spiritual spheres. If we fail to do so, human life will be against the laws of nature and will be doomed to self-destruction. This requires governments in each country to pursue appropriate environmental policies. These include:

- Love and protection of water, air, soil, animals and plants,

- Improvement and development of environmental protection services,

- Appropriate waste policy and waste-free environment.

- Improving the development of environmental protection services,

- Appropriate waste policy and waste-free environment

- Waste policy to prevent environmental pollution,

- Special attention should be paid to environmental education.

Ecological education needs a comprehensive educational policy that introduces the nature of nature, the laws of nature, and teaches that people should live under this law. The purpose of an ecological education is to make people understand that there is no life without nature. Mutually beneficial "cooperation" between nature and man is possible when everyone has a basic philosophical education about nature, society and man from an early age. Nature is the basic environment for the development of both the human body and the mind. Social material wealth cannot be imagined without food and nature. In a consumer-oriented, profit-driven market society, nature and man are at odds. This requires us to radical change our relationship with nature. In the name of resolving this relationship, a cruel policy of reducing the number of human beings is gaining ground. This is a good opportunity for the catastrophic policy of the same money owners, who want to deny the conscious action of man and make a profit between nature and man. It is no secret that they are directing natural disasters against humanity only in their interests. Then we need to challenge our Eternal Tengri philosophy against all of this. There is only one thing. That is Eternal Tengri – the Universe. Nature is the proof of the existence of the Eternal Heaven. There is no magic at all. Mongolians are intelligent people. But not so religious. Today, especially in the West, most people seem to be tired of religion. Religion requires us to believe in and worship God and mysticism. You don't have to be religious to be spiritual. So being religious and being spiritual are two different things. I think spirituality should be based on science. Because science answers what is based on evidence and spirituality answers what is real and important to us. Spirituality is inextricably linked with consciousness. To be spiritual means to expand one's consciousness, to develop one's mind. From the point of view of Munkh Tengerism, spirituality means expanding one's mind by interacting with nature and joining nature. It is a state of mind that has a deep sense of nature and a sense of unity with nature in all its aspects. Such a state can be experienced by a religious person, a scientist, or an ordinary person. For example, anyone who sees the night sky is in an incomprehensible state of mind. The moment our minds expand, marvel, and admire is a manifestation of our spirituality! The closer we are to nature, the deeper we can penetrate life and the more we can penetrate the mysteries of the universe, religious, secular, scientific and unconscious. The most important thing is to feel one with the whole universe. What exactly does it mean to be united with Eternal Heaven and Nature?

The individual is a unique being, as well as a "political animal" under the influence of society, the environment, and the noosphere. The individual must first and foremost unite with himself. The sages of the West and the East have been commanding through the millennia, "Know yourself." This is the basic condition of human spirituality. Let's not forget that we also have the secrets of the universe. Therefore, self-knowledge is the necessary basis for being spiritual. We also need to live in harmony with our society. This is another requirement of spirituality. It shows how important ethics and morality are here. We do not live outside society. We need love and care. It is also a law of social life for us to unite with a group, family, or community and meet each other's needs. It also requires us to be spiritual. We must also unite with the environment and protect it. It is also a manifestation of spirituality. The science of eco-psychology, which studies how humans interact with nature, has only recently emerged. A spiritual attitude towards nature should be a very important part of our spiritual life. Nature feeds us, clothes us, and provides us with all kinds of material things.

We need nature, nature doesn't need us. It leads mankind to respect nature and to recognize nature as sacred. We need to realize that we are one with the universe through nature. We strive for a deeper understanding of our place and position in the universe. It makes us interact with each other and with nature and marvels at the mysteries of the universe. There are many different doctrines, religions, and philosophies on this subject, and we must pay more attention to the evidence. Some are true and convincing, while others are full of deception and delusion.

In the depths of the universe, everything that happens internally is manifested through nature. There is no way to explain them outside of nature. There is no reality or magical world other than nature. Our bodies are also created by nature and are an integral part of nature.

The closest cognitive tool to nature is science. There is no such thing as magic in science.

But we should always keep in mind that the name of science is still misleading! Since it is based on evidence, our worldview, Eternal Tengri, becomes a philosophy of nature. It will be a broader and deeper meditation on our nature and its nature. Of course, theories about nature cannot be simply negotiated, coined, and coerced. This should be the new spiritual philosophy of the modern Mongolian nation. Munkh Tengerism is based on modern scientific knowledge and can be further developed. Therefore, it cannot be a religion.

I do not doubt that the Mongolian philosophy of eternal life, as a whole, will emerge as a whole. It is, of course, a philosophy that says that the peace of all human beings begins with a love of life and the protection of the environment. A person's spirituality includes his life, consciousness, will, and thoughts. All of this is also an integral part of Munkh Tengri. If the mind is consciousness, then the deepening of consciousness is the development of spirituality. Mindfulness is synonymous with consciousness. Spirituality is a state of consciousness that is expanded, deepened, developed, and strengthened. Some scholars have come to understand spirituality as "spiritual." It is better to be spiritual, because "spirituality" can be taken to mean mysticism or occultism. It separates the human body and mind, and it leads to superstition. Some spirituality is religious. Religion is the opposite of spirituality, and most spirituality is the opposite of religion. Spirituality is the expansion and deepening of consciousness. It is the realization that we have a deep relationship with reality and are closely connected with it. For Mongolians, that reality is the Eternal Heaven. The only thing that realizes its existence is Mother Nature. Our consciousness is linked to our emotions. Surprise, admiration, and joy are manifestations of a changed state of consciousness.

A changed state of consciousness means a sense of being united with infinite reality through meditation and other techniques to develop one's spirituality. It expands and deepens our minds and brings us to a new level of consciousness. It is our spiritual experience and will remain with us for a long time. In this way, we open the door to understand what is most important in life and enter into the essence of reality. In spiritual terms, power, wealth, and fame become nothing. Spirituality, first of all, leads us to put an end to the destructive and utilitarian use of the things around us. Thousands of years of our way of life and history have shown that those who worship, believe in, and admire the Eternal Tengri are not in a hostile relationship with nature. Since nature is the most important thing in life for us, our spirituality must also be based on nature. Munkh Tengerism is a philosophy of nature and about nature. And it is about the invaluable value of nature. There is no doubt that the Eternal Tengerianists has a broader and deeper belief in seeing and understanding nature. The question then arises as to how such a person can be created. First of all, our traditional spiritual practice is as useful as shamanism, meditation, and worship. It was a basic technique of nomadic civilization that had been tested for centuries to expand the mind. It is a powerful spiritual technique that has nothing to do with the teachings of religions that are detached from life. Nature is a sacred world. This is the manifestation and life of the Eternal Heaven. We are an integral part of nature. Nature is our home, the source of our true nature. Only a person who understands and feels this way can become a worshiper of Eternal Tengri. Worship means being in a relationship with Tengri.

For me, one morning I became a believer, worshiper, and philosopher of Eternal Heaven, but I looked for evidence first. Over the years of searching, learning, and study, I have come to realize that Munkh Tengerism is a very correct view of the world.

I wanted to share this knowledge with you. It is the result of my knowledge that it can be a philosophy of life-based on scientific facts and spiritual practice. Munkh Tenger worldview must be based on evidence. Of course, all the laws of nature are proof of this. That's why the concept of magic is out of place. So we seem to be closer to calling nature "spiritual". This is the philosophy of worshipping nature and dealing with nature. Accepting nature as it is a very good approach to life. Human beings do not judge and criticize natural things when they observe and study them. It teaches us to do the same in life. Spirituality is basically "natural." Spiritual experience is formed only in the interaction with nature.

It is clear that the experience learned from nature is also an attitude towards society. This allows us to understand and interpret reality more deeply and broadly. Since the concept of Eternal Heaven is a reflection and spiritual practice on nature and the world that is affected by our five senses, it has no place in the concept of mysticism, gods, and demons.

If you are following a philosophical trend, you need to put it into practice. The knowledge that is not used in life is not knowledge! Knowledge is always proven by experiment and experience! In the depths of the universe, everything that happens internally is manifested through nature. There is no way to explain them outside of nature. There is no reality or magical world other than nature. It can also be considered as human psychology of dealing with nature. There is no difference between how we treat nature and how we treat ourselves. We must understand that nature is the best environment for our body, mind and spirit to be healthy. That's why he should be protected. If there is a God, it is the

Eternal Heaven. The creation of the Eternal Heaven is nature. We are a creation of nature. Therefore, the most divine thing is nature.

This is the power of Eternal Heaven. The power of Eternal Heaven is the power of Nature. That's why I'm writing the word "nature" in capital letters in this book. The words God, Universe, and Eternal Heaven are different words with the same meaning. The concepts of God and the Universe mean the same thing in terms of Eternal Tengri in the sense of great creativity, transformer and infinite power. Eternal Heaven is a unified universe. The universe is not a God in religion and similar ideologies. Since the universe and nature are divine to us Mongolians, it is not a lie to call our "God" Eternal Heaven. This is not just because it is called the universe; on the other hand, the concept of the universe has been strengthened as a concept in modern science (cosmology, astronomy, astrophysics, etc.).

Eternal Tengri is the concept of Spirituality and the conscious universe.

We are not limited to the concept of the universe, but also the concept of the mental universe. Although the universe and nature are real, our consciousness, arousal, mind, and feelings about them are expressed in the words divine. In other words, it is the world of the spirit. Mongolians call Eternal Heaven Father Sky, Nature - Mother Nature. It is through this understanding, perception, and feeling that we overcame a separate consciousness of reality and came to an idea of a unified world. Eternal Heaven is our Creator and Father. Nature is our mother who carries and nourishes us. Nature is a source of great energy.

That power is everywhere and in everything. Our consciousness is an integral part of Nature and the Eternal Tengri. In this sense, we are one with the Eternal Tengri and Nature. The universe – Eternal Tengri was not created by anyone or anything. It exists by itself and evolves by itself. Eternal Heaven is infinite in time and space, with no beginning and no end. Therefore, the personal notion of "God," whose origin and whereabouts are unknown, is meaningless. The reason why man believes in God is that when he sees and feels the universe, he feels that there is infinite power and infinite power beyond him. Different civilizations have different interpretations of this feeling. We know that no matter what religion you belong to, their beliefs, surprises, and fears come from nature. As long as the universe exists, we are constantly aware of its divinity. This divine revelation is from the Eternal Tengri. As long as the universe exists, we are constantly aware of its divinity. This divine feeling will be the basis of our Eternal Tengri vision and will last forever. The more we experience the divinity of nature, the more we will have a spiritual relationship with it. Eternal Tengri calls us to Nature. The way to re-establish a deep connection with nature is to go out into nature and meditate in the depths of nature. Meditation allows us to unite our body, mind, and spirit with the rhythm of nature.

Most importantly, any meditation helps us feel that we are an integral part of a whole. This book is not a meditation book, so this topic is not included here. Concluding Remarks Eternal Heaven is not just a general concept or ideology. It's not a religion, it's not a science, it's a philosophy of life. It should be a philosophical system based on evidence. Eternity (Munkh) means infinite in time, and heaven (Tengri) means infinite in space. This should be our philosophy to wake up and revive Mongolians. In this book, I want to remind you that our civilization, which is closer to nature, is the foundation for discovering the truth. Each individual and each nation has its philosophical worldview.

Mongolians see our world as our Eternal Tengri. It will be more promising because it came out of our soul. The monasticism and shamanism that we used to have are now done. Now we have an old but new philosophy that can meet the needs of our minds. Undoubtedly, this philosophy is a philosophy that unites Mongolians with the wisdom of our lives, the world of spirituality and religion. Munkh Tengerism is, of course, philosophy of coexistence with nature, of health, energy, and happiness. I wish that this is a philosophy to create and develop the Mongolian world and that it is a torch of spirit that will develop from generation to generation! Life as a whole is a process of change and renewal. There is no such thing as a standing curtain. Every challenge in life allows us to grow and improve.

For the last 300 to 400 years, we have been driven by very weak beliefs. Buddhism, socialism and capitalism. These ideas and "beliefs" have led us to decay. These were ideas that denied life, polluted the minds of Mongolians, and degraded their humanity. It can be said that these systems of ideas have made our minds sick. Therefore, our philosophy of Eternal Heaven will be the way to get rid of all this and become healthy. Neither Christianity nor Buddhism is in harmony with the nature of our minds, nor is it a belief or ideology that enslaves us.

Eternal Heaven is our "god," and Eternal Heaven's Power is our inner strength. This is where our moral foundations should come from. That morality will be the morality that Mongolians have in common with our true nature.

Nature Worshiping Mongol Life and Divine Existence

Munkh Tengri and the Power of the Eternal Tengri (Heaven) affect individuals, society, animals, plants, and all life in general. Life is always a process of overcoming adversity, a process between existence and non-existence. One is growth and development, the other is decline and extinction. Life as a whole is a manifestation of this law. Such a "choice" to overcome oneself, or to remain a tortoise, or even to perish slowly, is faced by all living beings. The basis of prosperity is the grace of Eternal Heaven's Power. The basis of the evolution of all living things is their inner creativity. The development of life is always a process of overcoming oneself, and one is constantly evolving towards one's weaknesses, more and more strength and creativity. Our present life is just one stage of our evolution. We will continue to evolve, change and improve indefinitely. We need to understand that the current life of Mongolians is the beginning of great progress. I fully believe in this. I hope that there will be a basic moral principle. People who are driven by such beliefs will have the opportunity to create a Heavenly Man – as Great Chinggis Khan. This is the Divine Presence of Mongolia.

A consumer society that weakens the body, mind, and spirit, and which values comfort and satiety, has deteriorated in all respects. The lower middle class promoted positions, corruption, and helpless victim morality. We need to break the regime they have established. Use them to revive other beliefs and morals of Heaven. At that time, creative society and social relations will be established in Mongolia, consisting of optimistic, divine, physically, mentally and intellectually capable citizens. The members of that society will worship only the Eternal Heaven, live under the power of the Eternal Heaven, respect Mother Nature, and live by the Creative Law of the Eternal Heaven. This will be our real Mongolian Life - Divine Existence!

THE END

About the author of this book

Erdenebat Zorig. Mongolian writer. Veteran journalist, publicist, translator and blogger.

Activist for intellectual freedom, true political democracy and social justice.

His first book on the concept of Eternal Heaven – Munkh Tengri was published in Mongolia in 1997 under the title "Under the Power of Eternal Heaven", and "Living Under the Power of Eternal Tengri" (Meditations on Mongolian Spiritual Philosophy) is his second book on the subject.